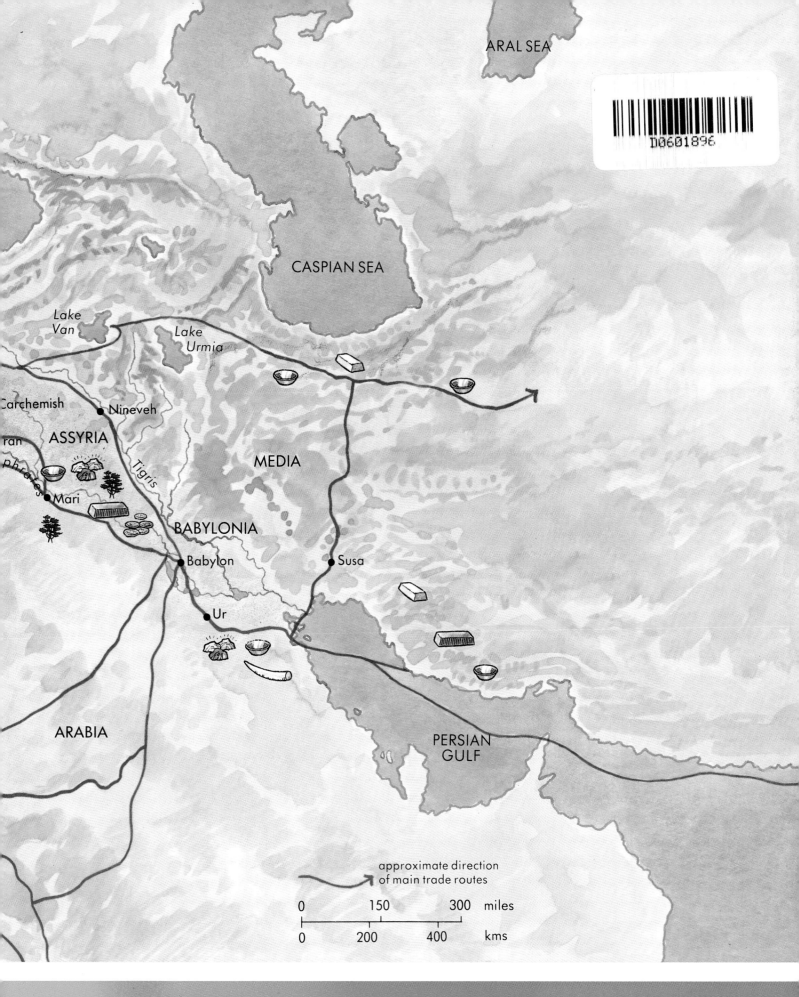

ARAL SEA

CASPIAN SEA

Lake
Van

Lake
Urmia

Carchemish

Nineveh

ASSYRIA

ran

phrates

MEDIA

Tigris

Mari

BABYLONIA

Babylon

Susa

Ur

ARABIA

PERSIAN
GULF

approximate direction
of main trade routes

0   150   300   miles

0   200   400   kms

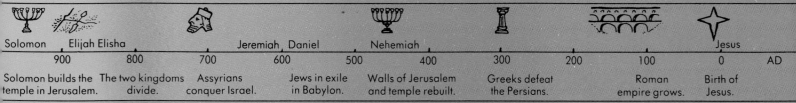

Solomon   Elijah Elisha   Jeremiah Daniel   Nehemiah   Jesus

900   800   700   600   500   400   300   200   100   0   AD

Solomon builds the   The two kingdoms   Assyrians   Jews in exile   Walls of Jerusalem   Greeks defeat   Roman   Birth of
temple in Jerusalem.   divide.   conquer Israel.   in Babylon.   and temple rebuilt.   the Persians.   empire grows.   Jesus.

Guide to the maps

Symbols

On the maps you will see small pictures or symbols that show where events happened or things came from. The key below shows what these mean.

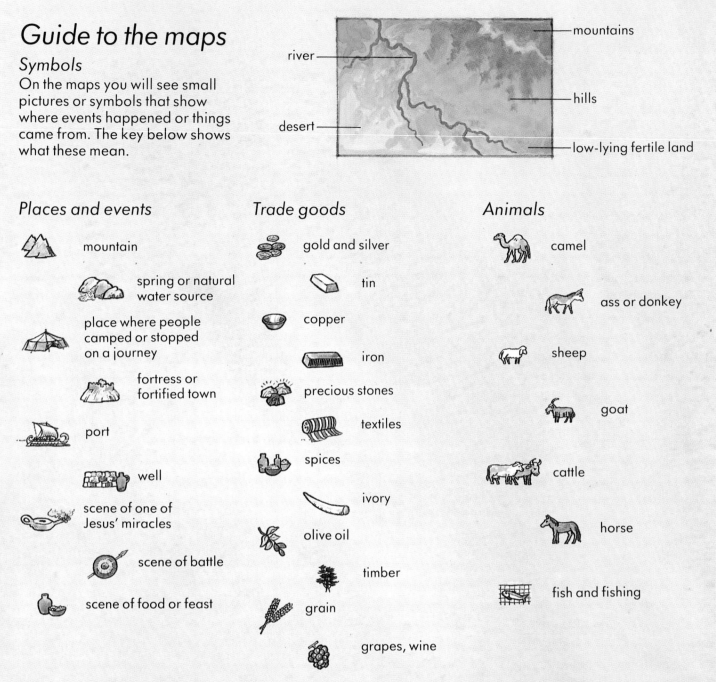

river
mountains
desert
hills
low-lying fertile land

Places and events

- mountain
- spring or natural water source
- place where people camped or stopped on a journey
- fortress or fortified town
- port
- well
- scene of one of Jesus' miracles
- scene of battle
- scene of food or feast

Trade goods

- gold and silver
- tin
- copper
- iron
- precious stones
- textiles
- spices
- ivory
- olive oil
- timber
- grain
- grapes, wine

Animals

- camel
- ass or donkey
- sheep
- goat
- cattle
- horse
- fish and fishing

Scale

On each of the large maps you will see a scale like this. This one means that 1 centimetre on the map stands for 100 kilometres on the land shown on the map.

| 0 | 150 | 300 | miles |
| 0 | 200 | 400 | kms |

Distance does not tell us very much unless we know how long it would take to get from one place to another. Remember that in Bible times there were no cars, trains or aeroplanes. The fastest that you could travel was on a horse, but not many people had these. Think about the farthest you have ever walked and how long it took. Then remember that the Bible people were often travelling with old people or young children. They often had sheep or goats with them, always straying from the path. How quickly do you think they could travel?

Time-lines and guide maps

The tiny guide maps and the time-lines for each chapter will help you to see when and where events happened. Compare them with the large maps and time-lines at the very beginning and end of the book to see how they fit into the whole picture.

Nehemiah

| 500 | 400 | 300 |

Walls of Jerusalem and temple rebuilt.

Greeks defeat the Persians.

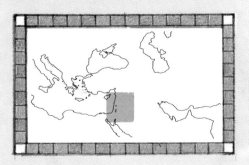

Children's ATLAS of the BIBLE

Written by Nicola Baxter

Consultant: Professor the Reverend R P Moss

Illustrated by Edgar Hodges

Contents

WORLD INTERNATIONAL PUBLISHING
MANCHESTER

Acknowledgements
The publishers wish to thank the following for permission to reproduce photographs:

The National Tourist Organisation of Greece (page 27);
The Egyptian State Tourist Office, London (page 11);
The Israel Government Tourist Office, London (pages 6 and 7);
The Italian State Tourist Office (E.N.I.T.), London (page 13); and
Peter Clayton (pages 14, 24 and 27).

Printed in Belgium

British Library Cataloguing in Publication Data
Baxter, Nicola
  Children's atlas of the bible.
  1. Middle East, ancient period. Historical sources: Bible
  – Maps, atlases
  I. Title   II. Hodges, Edgar, 1928–
  911.394

ISBN 0-7498-0183-2

In the beginning . . .

Genesis 1-8

The Bible starts by taking its readers back to the beginning of everything. It describes how God created the world and everything in it, including, last of all, human beings. The Bible tells us that God was pleased with everything He created, but that human beings were special. God put them in charge of everything on the earth. Today, we still have a responsibility to look after the world and not to destroy it by thoughtlessness or greed.

But the Bible describes how, even in the earliest times, people disobeyed God and spoiled their perfect world and their special closeness to Him. People were no longer perfectly happy, and before long their evil actions had become so great that God sent a great flood to clean the earth of their wickedness. But God did not want to destroy all His creation. He allowed one good man and his family to escape. This was Noah, his wife, their sons and their wives, who, following God's instructions, built an enormous boat, rather like a box, from wood and reeds. In this boat, or Ark, the family and one pair of each kind of animal on the earth lived safely for over a year, while the flood rose and fell. At the end of this time God put a rainbow in the sky as a promise that He would never again destroy the world by flooding.

The Old Testament stories take place over quite a small area of the world, in what we now call the Middle East.

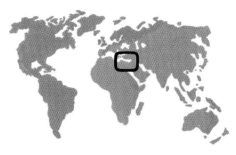

Looking after the world

Plants and animals are very important in the stories of the Bible – and not only because they provide food and drink, clothing, shelter, and wealth. They are also seen as evidence of God's presence in the world, and are able to show truths about God and about how people should live their lives.

The Bible is written in three languages and translators sometimes find it difficult to work out which animal is meant by a Hebrew, Aramaic or Greek word. Look at Deuteronomy 14: 4-5 in different Bible translations. Look at what the Bible says about the animals shown here, and see if you can work out

what characteristics the writers are thinking of. These animals were once common in Bible lands but are now rare or extinct there – because people, whom God put in charge of His creation, have hunted them or taken over their habitats.

Job 39: 6-8; Jeremiah 2: 24; 14: 6

Judges 14: 18; 1 Kings 7: 29; Isaiah 31: 4; 1 Peter 5: 8

Hosea 13: 7; Jeremiah 13: 23; Isaiah 11: 6

Job 39: 14-17; Lamentations 4: 3; Job 39: 18

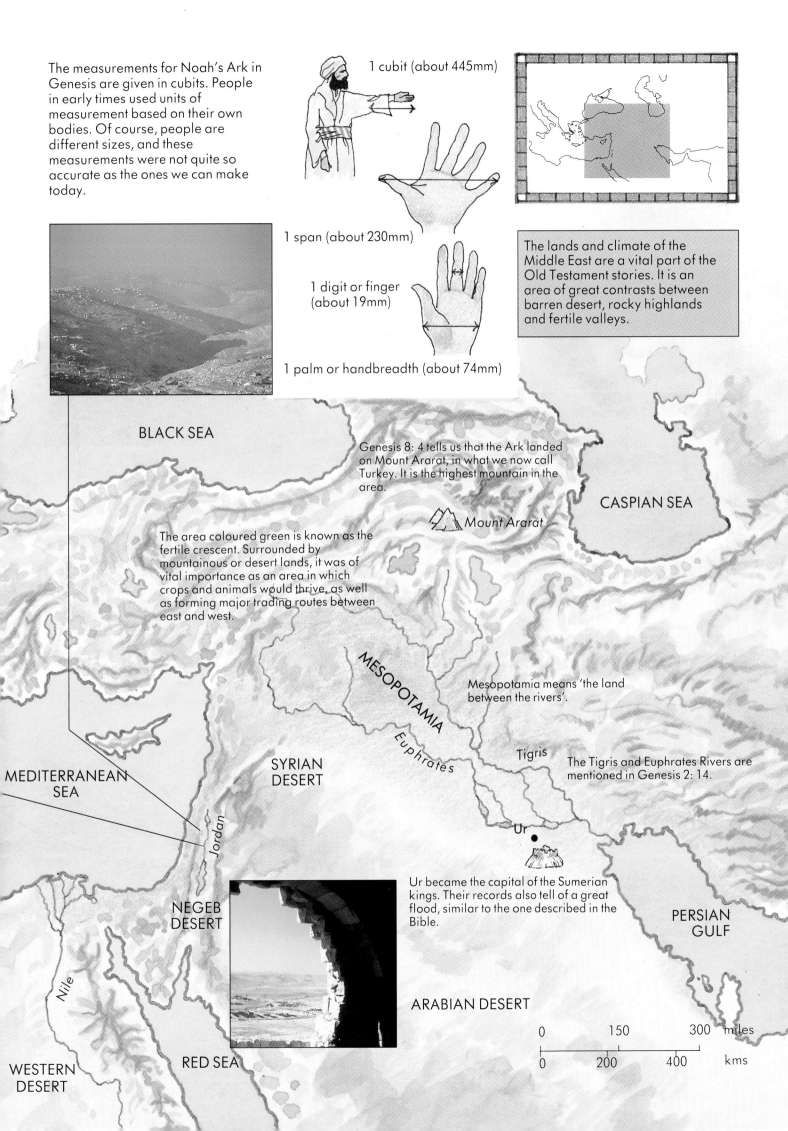

The measurements for Noah's Ark in Genesis are given in cubits. People in early times used units of measurement based on their own bodies. Of course, people are different sizes, and these measurements were not quite so accurate as the ones we can make today.

1 cubit (about 445mm)

1 span (about 230mm)

1 digit or finger (about 19mm)

1 palm or handbreadth (about 74mm)

The lands and climate of the Middle East are a vital part of the Old Testament stories. It is an area of great contrasts between barren desert, rocky highlands and fertile valleys.

BLACK SEA

Genesis 8: 4 tells us that the Ark landed on Mount Ararat, in what we now call Turkey. It is the highest mountain in the area.

Mount Ararat

CASPIAN SEA

The area coloured green is known as the fertile crescent. Surrounded by mountainous or desert lands, it was of vital importance as an area in which crops and animals would thrive, as well as forming major trading routes between east and west.

MESOPOTAMIA

Euphrates

Tigris

Mesopotamia means 'the land between the rivers'.

The Tigris and Euphrates Rivers are mentioned in Genesis 2: 14.

MEDITERRANEAN SEA

SYRIAN DESERT

Jordan

Ur

NEGEB DESERT

Ur became the capital of the Sumerian kings. Their records also tell of a great flood, similar to the one described in the Bible.

PERSIAN GULF

Nile

ARABIAN DESERT

0   150   300   miles

0   200   400   kms

WESTERN DESERT

RED SEA

Abraham and Isaac

Genesis 12-27

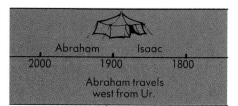

Abraham   Isaac

2000   1900   1800

Abraham travels
west from Ur.

After the stories of the creation of the world and the lives of people in early times, the Bible writers focus on one family – the family of Abraham. God promised Abram, as he was known at first, that he would lead him to a new country, and that his descendants would become a great nation. Abram followed God's instructions and travelled to Canaan. He was forced by famine to move for a while to Egypt, where he became rich. Later he returned to Canaan and settled at Hebron. Abram did not travel alone; with him were his wife, Sarai, his nephew, Lot, and many servants and slaves. When they returned to Canaan, Lot and Abram split up, so that they both had room to settle.

Abram and Lot had been living as nomads, travelling with their flocks and herds from place to place. But the area to which they came was already settled, with towns and local kings. In a war between these kings, Lot and his family were captured. Abram fought these kings and freed Lot. It was hard for Abram to see how God's promise could come true, for he had no land that was truly his, and he had no children.

But God repeated His promise to Abram and renamed him and his wife Abraham and Sarah. Very late in life, Sarah had a son, Isaac. When the boy was still young, God tested Abraham by asking him to sacrifice his only son. Abraham showed his obedience to God by preparing to do so, but God sent a ram to be killed instead. Isaac married Rebecca, and in time she gave birth to twins: Esau and Jacob. After his father's death, Isaac became rich and powerful, but his sons were great rivals. Although Esau was the elder, Jacob tricked Isaac into making him his heir.

Abram was born in Ur, at a time when it was a very great city with magnificent buildings. The beautiful objects below were all found in excavations of Ur. Abram's travels following God's instructions seem even more courageous when we think of the settled life he left.

Throughout history, there have been difficulties when nomadic peoples and settled peoples have occupied the same land. Abraham and his family were rich and powerful and able to pay their way. Local kings, like Abimelech, made treaties with them to make sure both sides benefited from their nearness. But water was very precious and liable to cause disputes, as we see in Genesis 21: 22-34 and 26: 12-35.

camel

goat

cattle

ass

sheep

Flocks and herds

Although we are told that Abraham owned gold and silver, his real wealth was in his animals, as it is for most nomadic people. He had large numbers of camels, goats, asses, cattle and sheep. Nomadic people need to travel in order to find new pastures for their animals. Close-grazing animals can do terrible damage to the environment if left too long in one place. The animals provide almost everything the people need: transport for themselves and their possessions; meat for food; milk to drink; skins and wool to make shoes, clothes and even homes – tents! Although Abraham and Isaac seem to have settled long enough in some places to plant and harvest crops, they still lived a mainly nomadic life.

Genesis 11: 1-9 tells the story of the tower of Babel. Men felt that if they worked together, there was nothing they could not achieve. To show their power, they began to build a city and an enormously high tower. The Bible tells us that God put an end to men's efforts to become all-powerful, by ensuring that people spoke different languages and could not understand each other. 'Babel' is probably Babylon, and the tower may well have been a ziggurat, or tower temple, like the one below.

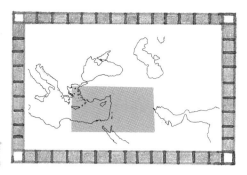

These tents, made of woven goat hair, are used by the Bedouin people today. Abraham's tents were probably very like this.

Abraham's journeys

Haran

PADDAN-ARAM

At a well in this area Abraham's servant meets Rebecca and knows that she should be Isaac's wife.

Euphrates

Tigris

BABYLONIA

Babylon

Ur

THE GREAT SEA
(Mediterranean Sea)

CANAAN

Abram stays here until famine makes him travel on to Egypt.

Shechem

Bethel

Hebron

Beersheba

The first time that Abraham owns land is when he buys a place near Hebron to bury Sarah.

At Beersheba Abraham has a dispute with the local king, Abimelech, about a well. Water was always likely to cause trouble between nomads and settled people.

NEGEB

EGYPT

Abram becomes wealthy in Egypt and leaves with large herds and flocks.

Nile

| 0 | | 150 | | 300 | miles |
| 0 | 200 | | 400 | | kms |

Jacob and Joseph

Genesis 28-50

After he had tricked his brother Esau out of his inheritance, Jacob went to visit his mother's family at Paddan-aram. As soon as he arrived he knew that he wanted to marry his cousin, Rachel, but in her father, Laban, Jacob met his match. He worked for Laban for twenty years in all, and was tricked into marrying Rachel's elder sister, Leah, as well as Rachel. Neither the two women nor Jacob were always happy. In the end Jacob returned to Canaan, with his wives, twelve children, and the flocks and herds that he had earnt in his years of work for Laban.

The homecoming might have been difficult, but Esau had forgiven his brother and was now living in Edom. At Bethel, God told Jacob that the promises He had made to Abraham would still come true. Jacob would be the father of a great nation, and from now on he would be called Israel.

However, Jacob's experiences do not seem to have taught him the wisdom of treating people fairly. He made no secret of the fact that Rachel's sons, Joseph and Benjamin, were his favourites. This, combined with the fact that Joseph had dreams that seemed to suggest that he was destined for better things than his brothers, caused ill-feeling. Finally, when they were away from home looking after the flocks, Joseph's brothers sold him into slavery, telling his father that he had been killed by a wild animal.

Joseph was taken to Egypt, where he had mixed fortunes until the Pharaoh had two dreams which his advisers were unable to explain to him. Joseph was able to interpret the dreams correctly: there would be seven good years in Egypt, followed by seven years of famine. Joseph was able to advise the Pharaoh how to manage this crisis, so that a potential disaster was turned to the Pharaoh's profit. Joseph became a very powerful man.

The famine that hit Egypt also affected Canaan. Hearing that there was grain in Egypt, Jacob sent some of his sons to buy food. It was some time before Joseph revealed his identity, but eventually Jacob and all his family came to live in Egypt under Joseph's protection. It was to be a long time before the people of Israel returned to Canaan.

Jacob gave Joseph a special coat to show his great love for him. Early translations of the Bible said that the coat was multi-coloured but scholars now think that the words may mean that the coat was long, with sleeves. In fact, if it was a special coat, the wool in it was probably dyed in different colours: red, blue and, most expensive of all, purple. Ordinary clothes were in the colours naturally found in wool: white, brown and black.

Grain from Egypt

The Egyptians made the most of their special climate and land. Every year in July tropical rains made the waters of the River Nile rise and flood its valley. By the end of October the waters had gone down, leaving behind a layer of rich mud, washed down from the mountains of Ethiopia. The combination of this fertile soil, water from the Nile and warm temperatures meant that the Egyptians could grow enormous amounts of grain and other foods. They made the most of the water by digging irrigation channels. However, the Nile flood was not very reliable. Some years it was not enough and some years there was too much water, causing great damage. Either of these could cause a famine like that of Joseph's time.

Egyptian farmers at work.

Life in the Egyptian court, as Joseph knew it, was rich and comfortable. It must have been a great contrast to the shepherd's life that he had known before.

The Egyptians believed that after death a person would need many of the things that he or she had used in life – including his or her body! Bodies were preserved, or embalmed, using salt and spices, then wrapped in cloth and put in a wooden coffin. Joseph's body was embalmed in this way.

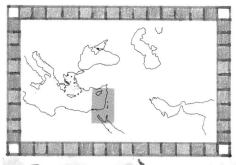

The journeys of Jacob and Joseph

THE GREAT SEA
(Mediterranean Sea)

Haran
Jacob meets his cousin Rachel at a well and wants to marry her.

PADDAN-ARAM

Jacob and his family leave Laban secretly, taking with them the flocks that Jacob has earnt in return for his work.

Jacob's journeys

Joseph's journeys

Esau's journeys

Joseph's brothers sell him to traders travelling from Gilead to Egypt with spices.

Dothan
Succoth
GILEAD
Mahanaim
Penuel
Jordan

Jacob dreams of a ladder with angels reaching to heaven. God tells him that His promises to Abraham are still true.

Shechem
Bethel
Ephrath

Esau comes to meet Jacob on his journey home.

Rachel dies giving birth to Benjamin and is buried at Ephrath (Bethlehem).

Jacob arrives at Hebron in time to see his father, Isaac, before he dies.

Hebron

SALT SEA

CANAAN

Beersheba

EDOM

Esau settles in Edom and his descendants are the Edomites.

GOSHEN

NEGEB DESERT

0   20   40   60 miles
0   20 40 60 80 100 kms

On

Nile

Joseph marries the daughter of an Egyptian priest.

The escape from Egypt

Exodus; Leviticus; Numbers; Deuteronomy

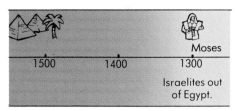
The people of Israel spent over 400 years in Egypt, where they grew into a large and powerful nation. The Pharaoh was afraid they would take control of Egypt, so he made them slaves, hoping to break their spirit. When the numbers of Israelites continued to increase, the Pharaoh ordered that every male Hebrew baby should be drowned at birth.

One woman was determined to save her child. She hid him in the reeds beside the River Nile, where he was found by the Pharaoh's daughter. She brought him up as a privileged Egyptian and called him Moses. Moses' life could not have been more different from that of a slave, but he knew who his people were. One day, when he was grown up, he killed an Egyptian who was mistreating a Hebrew slave. His crime was discovered and he was forced to flee to Midian, where he married and had a son.

However, God had not forgotten His promise to give His chosen people a land of their own. He told Moses to go back to Egypt and lead his people to freedom. Moses was doubtful but, helped by his brother Aaron, he set about the task.

Of course, the Pharaoh was unwilling to let the Hebrews go. So God sent ten plagues on Egypt and in the last one the firstborn child of every Egyptian family was killed one night. By following God's instructions, the Hebrews avoided this dreadful fate, and before daybreak they had set off on their great journey.

The probable route of their exodus (which means 'going out') from Egypt is shown on the map. It was not an easy journey – the people were going into the unknown and were often afraid and confused. In the end, they spent over 40 years in the wilderness, and most of the people who left Egypt failed to enter the promised land, including Moses. Before he died, however, he named Joshua as the next leader.

On Mount Sinai God gave the Ten Commandments to Moses for the people to follow. He made a kind of contract (a covenant) with them to show that they were His chosen people. There were many times on the journey when the people became confused and did wrong things. God gave them laws, so that they would know how He wanted them to live. He also gave Moses hundreds of rules about how to live and worship. Some of these rules were about food, as you can read below. Exodus, Numbers, Deuteronomy and Leviticus give these and other laws in great detail.

You must have no god other than Me.

You must not worship any carved image.

You must not use My name carelessly.

You must not work on the Sabbath day, which should be a special, holy day.

Treat your father and mother with honour and respect.

Kill no one.

Do not sleep with another man's wife, or another woman's husband.

Do not steal.

Do not tell lies.

Do not long for anything that belongs to someone else.

Exodus 20: 1-17; Deuteronomy 5: 6-21

unclean

clean

The food laws

As well as giving Moses laws about how to worship, how to organize the people, and what to do if they became ill, God told him what they could and could not eat. Animals, birds and fish were divided into 'clean' and 'unclean'. You can see some examples here and in Leviticus 11: 12-47 and Deuteronomy 14: 3-21. God also gave instructions about how other kinds of food were to be prepared. Why God decided that His people should not eat certain foods is not clear. Some people think it was for reasons of hygiene on the difficult journey. It may also have been to prevent cruelty to animals. Many Jewish people today still follow these laws. They call food which they can eat kasher or kosher.

On the night that the firstborn children of the Egyptian families were killed, the people of Israel followed God's instructions and prepared a special meal. This is called the Passover because death 'passed over' the homes of the people of Israel. To this day Jews all over the world commemorate that night and their freedom from slavery by eating a Passover meal on the anniversary of the event. The Passover has a special meaning for Christians, too, because the last supper that Jesus ate with His disciples, telling them to remember Him with bread and wine, was a Passover meal.

Exodus 12: 12 – 13: 10; Mark 14: 12-31

The probable route that the people of Israel took on their journey from Egypt to Canaan. (Exodus gives a detailed list of the places visited, but today it is hard to be sure where they were.)

THE GREAT SEA
(Mediterranean Sea)

God did not lead the people of Israel all the way to the promised land by the shortest route, along the road to the land of the powerful Philistines, for He thought they would get discouraged if they had to fight battles too soon.

road to the land of the Philistines

Mount Nebo

Jericho

CANAAN

MOAB

SALT SEA
(Dead Sea)

The king of Moab will not let the people of Israel cross his land.

Rameses

GOSHEN

Succoth

Pithom

Bitter Lakes

The people of Israel cross the Sea of Reeds but the Pharaoh's army is drowned.

WILDERNESS OF SHUR

NEGEB DESERT

Kadesh-barnea

EDOM

The king of Edom will not let the people of Israel cross his land.

EGYPT

Moses sends 12 men to reconnoitre the land of Canaan. Only two, Joshua and Caleb, want to go on. The report of the other 10 makes some of the people want to turn back. As a punishment God makes the people of Israel spend the next 40 years in the wilderness.

WILDERNESS OF PARAN

SINAI

Ezion-geber

Nile

God sends down manna – a mysterious food for His people.

WILDERNESS OF SIN

Moses makes water flow from a rock.

God gives Moses the Ten Commandments.

Rephidim

Mount Sinai (Mount Horeb)

MIDIAN

The people of Israel needed a safe place to keep all God's laws on their journey, so God gave them detailed instructions for a chest to carry them in. This was called the Ark of the Covenant.

Exodus 25: 10-22; Deuteronomy 10: 1-5

The people of Israel fight the Amalekites and win.

| 0 | 20 | 40 | 60 | miles |
| 0 | 20 | 40 | 60 | 80 | 100 | kms |

SEA OF REEDS
(Red Sea)

The promised land

Joshua; Judges

When the people of Israel reached Canaan, they could not simply move in and occupy the land. As in the time of Abraham, the land was already settled, with towns and local kings. There were too many Israelites to live alongside the local people, and in any case, God had promised them that the land would be their own. What the people of Israel needed was a great military leader, and Joshua proved to be just that.

After crossing the River Jordan, the Israelites began a series of battles to capture important Canaanite settlements. First they won Jericho and Ai. News of these victories reached other parts of Canaan and local kings from the south agreed to band together to attack the newcomers. When the Israelites had defeated these kings, a new alliance in the north had to be defeated too. Although there were still many Canaanite settlements left, Joshua divided the land between the tribes. Before he died, Joshua warned the Israelites to stay true to their God and not to be tempted to follow the customs and gods of the Canaanites. Despite Joshua's warning, the Israelites found it hard to keep faith with God during the years that followed, which is called the time of the 'judges'. The Israelites stopped following God's laws; their enemies overwhelmed them; a 'judge' arose who fought the enemies and reminded the Israelites of God's purpose: this pattern was repeated over and over again. One of the best known of these judges was Samson. The judges did not always act in an honourable or law-abiding way, but what they had in common was an unswerving faithfulness to God. The last judge, Samuel, led the way to a new stage in the history of the Israelites.

The first major battle was for control of Jericho, an important city. Following instructions from God, the army marched round it for six days, blowing rams' horns like the ones above. On the seventh day, after marching round seven times, the army gave a great shout and took the city through the breaking down of the walls. Some people have suggested that the marching somehow weakened the walls of the city. A war of nerves was in progress. The steady tramping outside and the suspense of wondering when the attack would happen must have unnerved the people of Jericho.

The fruit of the land

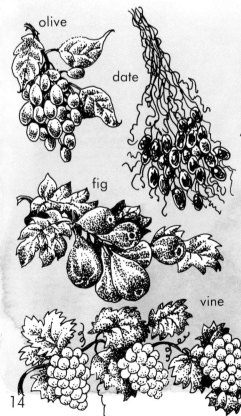

olive

date

fig

vine

The people of Israel were told that the promised land was a fruitful one. Fruiting trees are often mentioned in the Bible, often as examples of God's generosity and faithfulness. The olive was important because the fruits were crushed to provide oil. This was used in cooking, for burning in lamps and in religious ceremonies. As well as eating fresh or dried grapes from the vine, the Israelites fermented the juice of the fruit to make wine. This was their normal drink. Dates and figs could also be eaten fresh or dried — especially useful for carrying on journeys in a hot country where it was difficult to keep foods for long.

Several of the cities of Canaan have been excavated in recent years. The photograph above shows Jericho. Although ancient walls of Jericho and evidence of a fire in the city have been found, they may well be earlier than the time of Joshua. Very little is known about the city that Joshua would have seen.

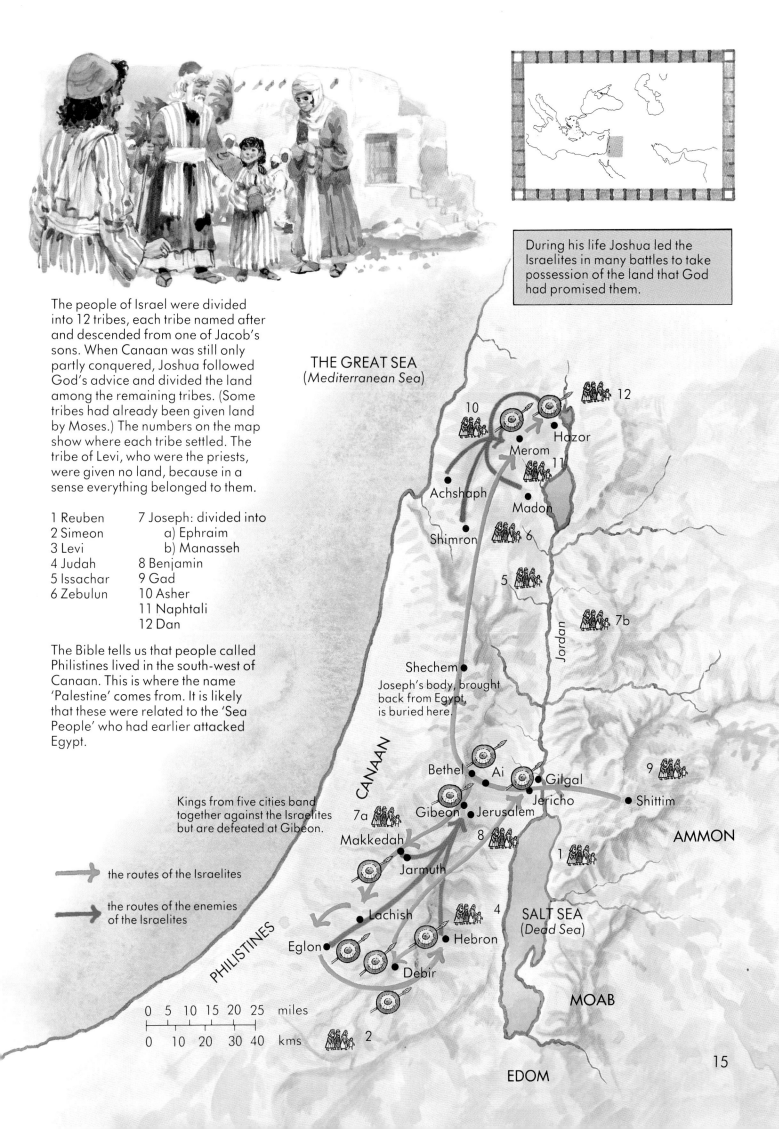

The people of Israel were divided into 12 tribes, each tribe named after and descended from one of Jacob's sons. When Canaan was still only partly conquered, Joshua followed God's advice and divided the land among the remaining tribes. (Some tribes had already been given land by Moses.) The numbers on the map show where each tribe settled. The tribe of Levi, who were the priests, were given no land, because in a sense everything belonged to them.

1 Reuben
2 Simeon
3 Levi
4 Judah
5 Issachar
6 Zebulun
7 Joseph: divided into
  a) Ephraim
  b) Manasseh
8 Benjamin
9 Gad
10 Asher
11 Naphtali
12 Dan

The Bible tells us that people called Philistines lived in the south-west of Canaan. This is where the name 'Palestine' comes from. It is likely that these were related to the 'Sea People' who had earlier attacked Egypt.

During his life Joshua led the Israelites in many battles to take possession of the land that God had promised them.

THE GREAT SEA
(Mediterranean Sea)

Hazor
Merom
Achshaph
Madon
Shimron
Jordan
Shechem
Joseph's body, brought back from Egypt, is buried here.

Kings from five cities band together against the Israelites but are defeated at Gibeon.

Bethel
Ai
Gilgal
Gibeon
Jerusalem
Jericho
Shittim
Makkedah
Jarmuth
Lachish
Hebron
Eglon
Debir

AMMON

SALT SEA
(Dead Sea)

MOAB

EDOM

CANAAN

PHILISTINES

the routes of the Israelites

the routes of the enemies of the Israelites

0 5 10 15 20 25 miles
0 10 20 30 40 kms

15

The first kings of Israel

1 and 2 Samuel; 1 Kings 1-11; 2 Chronicles 1-9

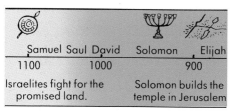

	Samuel Saul David	Solomon	Elijah
	1100	1000	900
	Israelites fight for the promised land.	Solomon builds the temple in Jerusalem	

Samuel was brought up to serve God in the tabernacle, or 'tent of worship', at Shiloh. He became a respected judge over Israel, but the people did not follow God faithfully, even after God helped them to defeat the attacking Philistines. When Samuel grew old, the people asked him to appoint a king to govern them and fight for them. They seemed to feel that this would be better and easier than living under the rule of God. Samuel tried to explain that a king would make demands on them as well as helping them, but they would not change their minds.

So Samuel anointed king a man called Saul from the tribe of Benjamin. Saul and his son Jonathan led the Israelites in many battles against the Philistines and other neighbouring peoples. But although Saul was a successful military leader, he began to think more of the riches he captured and of his own importance than of God. God told Samuel to find another king and he found David, the son of Jesse, from Bethlehem, while Saul was still alive.

David served in Saul's household and gained a reputation as a great soldier. He became more popular than Saul and a great friend of Saul's son, Jonathan. But Saul hated David and tried to kill him. David lived in hiding for some time. In the end both Saul and his son were killed in battle, and David became king of Israel.

David's military skill was much needed. He expanded the kingdom and defeated many enemies. He made Jerusalem the capital city and left a strong kingdom to his son, Solomon. Solomon's reign was a prosperous one for Israel. From a position of strength, Solomon made profitable alliances with his neighbours. He made the most of Israel's position on many trade routes. But foreign customs and religions as well as goods moved through the kingdom. Even Solomon was not faithful to God at the end of his life.

1 Kings 5-7 and 2 Chronicles 2-4 tell of the magnificence of the temple that Solomon built in Jerusalem. This temple was not like a huge cathedral for the people, but a very richly decorated 'home' for the Ark of the Covenant, where the priests and the king could worship God. The descriptions suggest that it may have looked like this.

Saul suffered from an illness that was soothed when David played the harp to him. Harps are mentioned often in the Old Testament and were probably like the one below. David's harp was made of cypress wood. David first became famous as a soldier when he killed Goliath, a Philistine. Goliath was nearly three metres (nine feet) tall, and much stronger than David. But David was able to kill Goliath from a distance by skilfully using a sling before Goliath could reach him.

cedar of Lebanon

oak

pine

olive

Timber and trees

Solomon imported a great deal of timber for his great building projects. Cedar wood came from Lebanon. It was cut into logs and floated down the coast. Today, very few trees are left of the great forests of Lebanon. Pine also came from Lebanon by the same means. Olive wood was used for finer carving. Also used was 'almug wood' which may have been sandalwood. Oak trees once grew thickly on the hillsides in Palestine. It was in an oak tree that Absalom, David's rebellious son, was caught before his death.

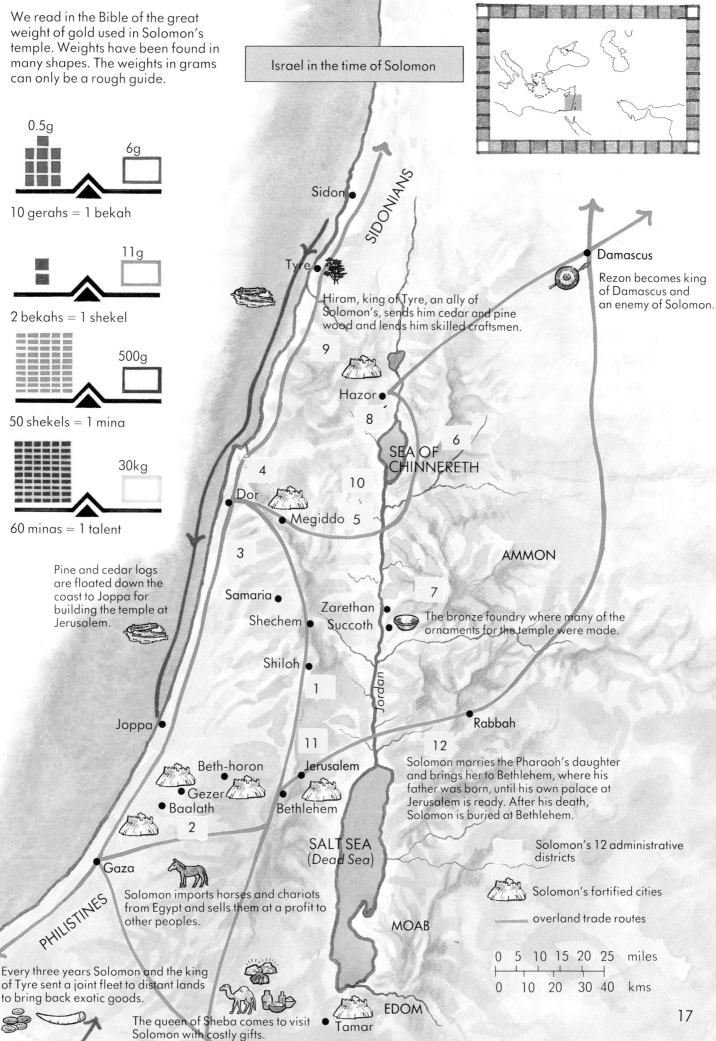

We read in the Bible of the great weight of gold used in Solomon's temple. Weights have been found in many shapes. The weights in grams can only be a rough guide.

0.5g
6g
10 gerahs = 1 bekah

11g
2 bekahs = 1 shekel

500g
50 shekels = 1 mina

30kg
60 minas = 1 talent

Israel in the time of Solomon

Sidon

SIDONIANS

Tyre

Damascus

Rezon becomes king of Damascus and an enemy of Solomon.

Hiram, king of Tyre, an ally of Solomon's, sends him cedar and pine wood and lends him skilled craftsmen.

9

Hazor

8

6

SEA OF CHINNERETH

4

10

Dor

Megiddo   5

3

AMMON

Pine and cedar logs are floated down the coast to Joppa for building the temple at Jerusalem.

Samaria

Shechem

Zarethan
Succoth

7

The bronze foundry where many of the ornaments for the temple were made.

Shiloh

1

Jordan

Joppa

11

Rabbah

12

Beth-horon

Gezer

Baalath

Jerusalem

Bethlehem

2

Solomon marries the Pharaoh's daughter and brings her to Bethlehem, where his father was born, until his own palace at Jerusalem is ready. After his death, Solomon is buried at Bethlehem.

Gaza

PHILISTINES

Solomon imports horses and chariots from Egypt and sells them at a profit to other peoples.

SALT SEA
(Dead Sea)

Solomon's 12 administrative districts

Solomon's fortified cities

overland trade routes

MOAB

0 5 10 15 20 25 miles

0   10   20   30 40 kms

Every three years Solomon and the king of Tyre sent a joint fleet to distant lands to bring back exotic goods.

The queen of Sheba comes to visit Solomon with costly gifts.

EDOM

Tamar

The division of Israel

1 Kings 12-22; 2 Kings 1-19; 2 Chronicles 10-32; Isaiah

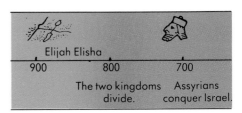

Solomon's son, Rehoboam, was not as wise a ruler as his father. Soon after he became king his own people turned against him, and the kingdom was split into Israel in the north and Judah in the south. Israel was ruled by Jeroboam, who had been exiled in Egypt by Solomon. Both Israel and Judah began to turn away from the worship of God and, as king after king ruled each kingdom, matters grew worse, although a few kings tried to lead the people back to God. In the reign of Ahab a prophet named Elijah warned against following other gods, especially Baal.

Meanwhile, Israel and Judah were under attack from Egypt in the south and Aram (Syria) in the north. Jehoshaphat of Judah and Ahab of Israel fought together to try to regain Ramoth-gilead in the east from the Syrians. After the death of Elijah, another prophet, Elisha, tried to keep the rulers and their people faithful to God.

Over the years, many nations attacked Judah and Israel. Sometimes they were successful for a while, only to be pushed back later. Sometimes the attacking king would go away if offered gold and silver. The kings of Judah and Israel were allies at times and enemies at others; many of them did not reign for very long. Throughout this period foreign gods were worshipped, often with the encouragement of the kings.

From the time of Ahab onwards one enemy came to be feared more than any other – the Assyrians. For a while the kings kept the Assyrians away by paying them. Prophets in this period, such as Jonah, Amos, Hosea and Isaiah, warned of the danger of turning away from God. Over a period of nearly one hundred and fifty years, the Assyrians overran first Israel and then Judah, and deported many of the Israelites.

The Old Testament has many stories of the temptation of the Israelites to turn from God to the worship of Baal, a Canaanite god. Baal was a weather god, believed to bring the rain and sun needed for crops. His symbol was a bull, which is why the people of Judah were very suspicious of the golden bulls set up by Jeroboam at Bethel and Dan.

Rulers of Israel

Jeroboam
Nadab
Baasha
Elah
Zimri
Omri
Ahab
Ahaziah
Jehoram
Jehu
Jehoahaz
Jehoash
Jeroboam
Zechariah
Shallum
Menahem
Pekahiah
Pekah
Hoshea
The Assyrians conquer Israel.

Rulers of Judah

Rehoboam
Abijam
Asa
Jehoshaphat
Joram
Ahaziah
Athaliah
Joash
Amaziah
Uzziah
Jotham
Ahaz
Hezekiah
Manasseh
Amon
Josiah
Jehoahaz
Jehoiakim
Jehoiachin
The Assyrians conquer Judah.
Zedekiah

collared dove

brown-necked raven

Egyptian vulture

golden eagle

Birds of the Bible

1 Kings 17: 4-6 tells how ravens brought food to Elijah. They appear several times in the Bible as signs of God's protection. Noah sent a raven out of the Ark. The dove, also sent out of the Ark, is the bird mentioned most often in the Bible. When Jesus was baptized, the spirit of God appeared in the shape of a dove. Some scholars think that the many references to eagles in the Bible are really about vultures. It is the bird's high and fast flight that is usually mentioned, and this could apply to both birds.

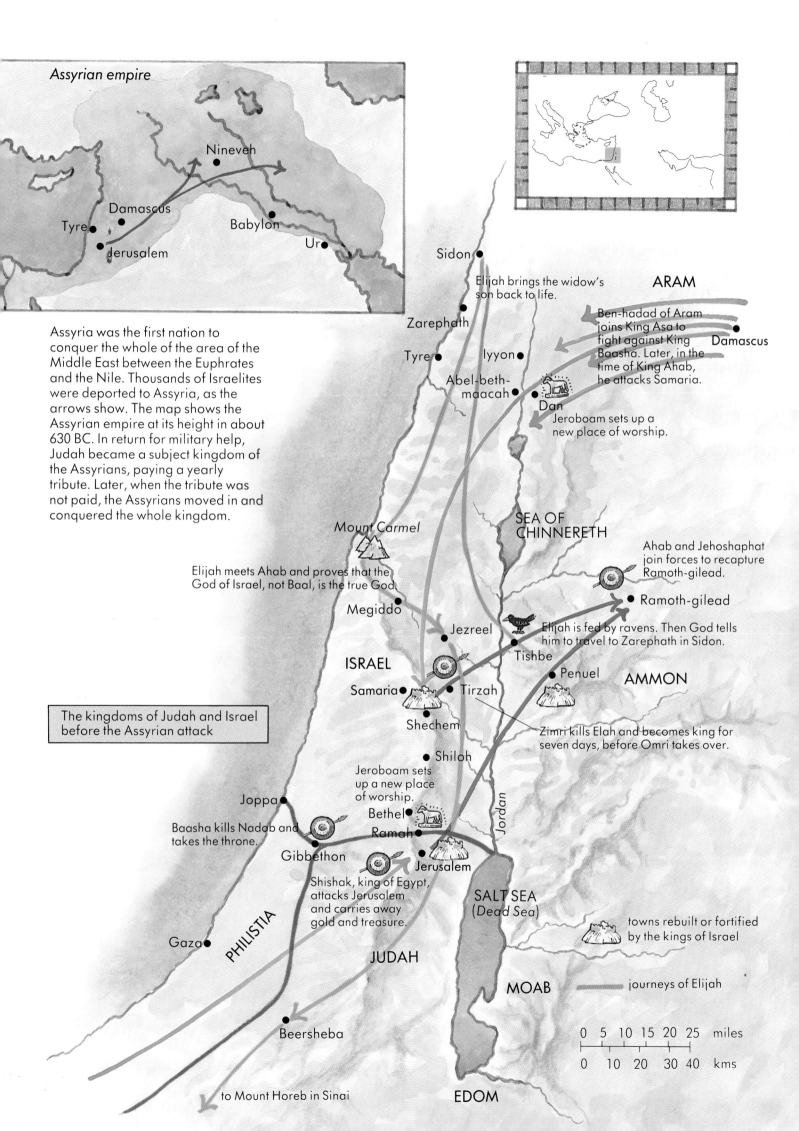

Assyrian empire

Nineveh

Damascus

Tyre

Babylon

Jerusalem

Ur

Assyria was the first nation to conquer the whole of the area of the Middle East between the Euphrates and the Nile. Thousands of Israelites were deported to Assyria, as the arrows show. The map shows the Assyrian empire at its height in about 630 BC. In return for military help, Judah became a subject kingdom of the Assyrians, paying a yearly tribute. Later, when the tribute was not paid, the Assyrians moved in and conquered the whole kingdom.

The kingdoms of Judah and Israel before the Assyrian attack

Sidon

Elijah brings the widow's son back to life.

ARAM

Zarephath

Ben-hadad of Aram joins King Asa to fight against King Baasha. Later, in the time of King Ahab, he attacks Samaria.

Damascus

Tyre

Iyyon

Abel-beth-maacah

Dan

Jeroboam sets up a new place of worship.

SEA OF CHINNERETH

Mount Carmel

Ahab and Jehoshaphat join forces to recapture Ramoth-gilead.

Elijah meets Ahab and proves that the God of Israel, not Baal, is the true God.

Megiddo

Ramoth-gilead

Jezreel

Elijah is fed by ravens. Then God tells him to travel to Zarephath in Sidon.

Tishbe

ISRAEL

Penuel

AMMON

Samaria

Tirzah

Shechem

Zimri kills Elah and becomes king for seven days, before Omri takes over.

Shiloh

Jeroboam sets up a new place of worship.

Joppa

Bethel

Baasha kills Nadab and takes the throne.

Ramah

Gibbethon

Jerusalem

Shishak, king of Egypt, attacks Jerusalem and carries away gold and treasure.

SALT SEA (Dead Sea)

Gaza

PHILISTIA

towns rebuilt or fortified by the kings of Israel

JUDAH

MOAB

journeys of Elijah

Beersheba

0 5 10 15 20 25 miles

0 10 20 30 40 kms

to Mount Horeb in Sinai

EDOM

Jordan

Exile and return

2 Kings 23: 28 – 25: 30; 2 Chronicles 35: 20 – 36: 23; Ezra; Nehemiah; Jeremiah 26-43, 52; Lamentations; Ezekiel; Daniel; Haggai; Zechariah

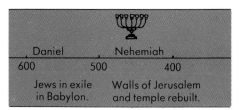

Daniel		Nehemiah	
600	500		400
Jews in exile in Babylon.		Walls of Jerusalem and temple rebuilt.	

Only a hundred years after the conquest of Israel, the Assyrian empire was itself attacked and conquered. Judah became a battleground, as the Egyptians from the west confronted the Babylonians from the east. The Jews were caught in the middle, either paying tribute to the larger powers or appealing for help from one to fight the other. Once again, prophets, such as Jeremiah, warned of the results of not being united in obeying God's laws.

Finally, Jerusalem was captured by the Babylonians, and all but the poorest people were deported to Babylon. The temple in Jerusalem was destroyed and its treasure taken. In Babylon the Jews were not harshly treated but allowed to follow their own customs and religion. But the loss of the promised land was a terrible shock. It made them think again about their relationship with God. Having lost the temple as a focus for worship, the Jews realized the importance of the written law. Just as in the time of Moses, it helped them to remember that they were still God's chosen people, although far from home. Both Daniel and Ezekiel reminded them that no earthly kingdom lasts for ever.

In fact, within 50 years of the fall of Jerusalem, the Babylonian empire had been conquered by the Persians, led by King Cyrus. Cyrus could not control his massive empire alone, so he set up provinces, each with its own ruler. He allowed the Jews to go back to Jerusalem and rebuild the temple, giving them money and the temple treasure to take with them.

The exiles who returned – for some of the Jews decided to settle in other parts of the Persian empire – were led by Zerubbabel, grandson of King Jehoiachin. Despite an enthusiastic start, work on the temple was slow. The builders had to be spurred on by Haggai and Zechariah. It was nearly a hundred years later that Nehemiah came from Susa to rebuild the walls and gates of Jerusalem.

It was during the exile in Babylon, when the written word of God took on a greater importance, that many of the Old Testament writings took the form that we know today. Jews divide these books into the Law, the Prophets and the Writings. These terms are sometimes used in the New Testament to describe the Old Testament. The oldest copies of these books discovered so far are those found in the Dead Sea caves in 1947. These date from the first century BC.

The probable stages in the building of Jerusalem. Much of the original city had to be rebuilt after the exile.

The shepherd's enemies

Syrian bear

Judaean wolf

lioness

Hosea 13 compares God's anger when his people disobey him to the fierceness of a bear or lioness. To people whose livelihood depended on flocks of sheep and goats, this was a powerful image. Even after the Jews were no longer nomads, these animals were of huge importance. Frequently in the Old and New Testaments wild animals that might threaten the shepherd's flocks, like the ones above, are mentioned as symbols of strength and destruction. Jesus was drawing on a long tradition when He described Himself as a good shepherd in John 10: 11-16.

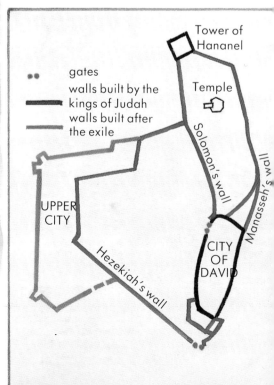

Tower of Hananel

gates

walls built by the kings of Judah

walls built after the exile

Temple

Solomon's wall

Manasseh's wall

UPPER CITY

CITY OF DAVID

Hezekiah's wall

20

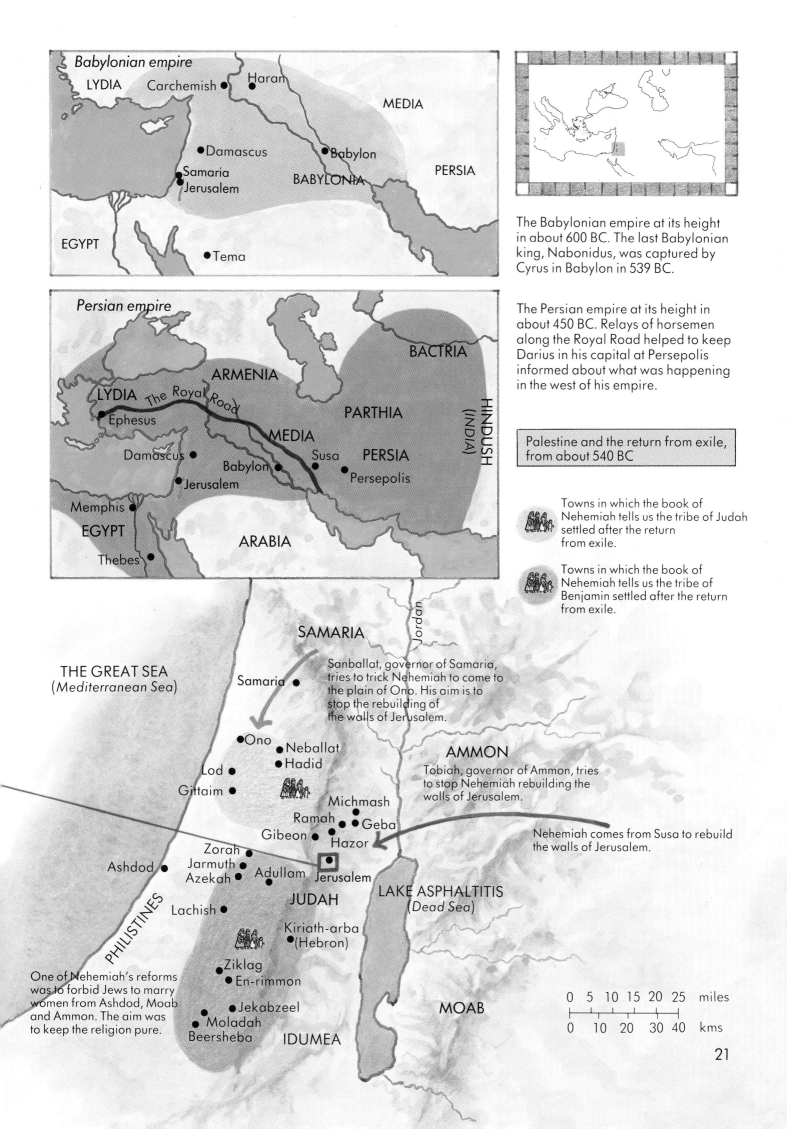

Babylonian empire

LYDIA
Carchemish • Haran
MEDIA
• Damascus
• Babylon
Samaria
Jerusalem
BABYLONIA
PERSIA
EGYPT
• Tema

The Babylonian empire at its height in about 600 BC. The last Babylonian king, Nabonidus, was captured by Cyrus in Babylon in 539 BC.

Persian empire

BACTRIA
ARMENIA
LYDIA The Royal Road
Ephesus
PARTHIA
MEDIA
HINDUSH (INDIA)
Damascus
Susa
Babylon
PERSIA
Jerusalem
Persepolis
Memphis
EGYPT
ARABIA
Thebes

The Persian empire at its height in about 450 BC. Relays of horsemen along the Royal Road helped to keep Darius in his capital at Persepolis informed about what was happening in the west of his empire.

Palestine and the return from exile, from about 540 BC

Towns in which the book of Nehemiah tells us the tribe of Judah settled after the return from exile.

Towns in which the book of Nehemiah tells us the tribe of Benjamin settled after the return from exile.

SAMARIA

Jordan

THE GREAT SEA
(Mediterranean Sea)

Samaria •

Sanballat, governor of Samaria, tries to trick Nehemiah to come to the plain of Ono. His aim is to stop the rebuilding of the walls of Jerusalem.

• Ono
• Neballat
Lod •
• Hadid
Gittaim •

AMMON

Tobiah, governor of Ammon, tries to stop Nehemiah rebuilding the walls of Jerusalem.

Michmash •
Ramah •
• Geba
Gibeon •
Hazor •

Nehemiah comes from Susa to rebuild the walls of Jerusalem.

Zorah •
Ashdod •
Jarmuth •
Azekah • Adullam •
Jerusalem
JUDAH

LAKE ASPHALTITIS
(Dead Sea)

PHILISTINES

Lachish •

Kiriath-arba
• (Hebron)

Ziklag •
• En-rimmon

One of Nehemiah's reforms was to forbid Jews to marry women from Ashdod, Moab and Ammon. The aim was to keep the religion pure.

• Jekabzeel
• Moladah
Beersheba •
IDUMEA

MOAB

0 5 10 15 20 25 miles

0 10 20 30 40 kms

21

The birth of Jesus

Matthew 1-2; Luke 1: 5 – 2: 20

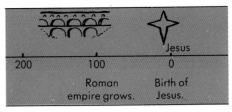

The power of the Persians was eventually broken by Greece. After years of conflict between the two nations, Alexander the Great finally conquered vast areas of the Middle East for Greece before his death in 323 BC. It was not just a military conquest. Alexander encouraged Greeks to settle throughout the empire, so that Greek life, thought, language and culture spread over a huge area. Later, it was in Greek that the New Testament was written.

Gradually, over the next three centuries, however, the Romans conquered most of the Greek empire and much beyond it. The Romans did not destroy everything that the Greeks valued, but added efficient systems of law and order, roads and water supplies. But ruling such a wide variety of peoples and countries was difficult and expensive. Roman soldiers were posted everywhere and taxes on local people were high. The Romans were far from popular.

Mary was a young girl living in Nazareth at the time of the Roman occupation. She was stunned to be told by an angel that she was pregnant and that her child would be the Son of God, but she was willing to do whatever God wanted. God made sure that Mary's fiancé, Joseph, understood that she was carrying a special child and their marriage went ahead.

When Mary was almost ready to give birth, a Roman census was announced. By gathering information about people the Romans could work out how best to govern them and how high to set the taxes. Mary and Joseph had to travel to Bethlehem for the census, because it was Joseph's birthplace. While they were there, Jesus was born, in very poor circumstances. Visits to the newborn baby by shepherds and later by wise men from the East, led by a strange star in the sky, showed that He was no ordinary child.

The Jews had been waiting for the arrival of the Messiah, a king descended from King David who would bring in an age in which the Jewish people would truly become the kingdom of God. Many Jews believed that this king would be a military leader who would defeat their Roman rulers. When the wise men told Herod the Great, the king of the Jews, about the star and the baby, he ordered the death of all children in Bethlehem under the age of two. Mary and Joseph escaped with the baby to Egypt, where Jesus spent His first years.

This Roman coin shows the head of Augustus, who was emperor of Rome when Jesus was born.

The Greek empire 250 years before the birth of Jesus.

Scents and spices

When the wise men from the East came to visit Jesus soon after His birth, they brought gifts of gold, frankincense and myrrh. Spices were important for flavouring and preserving food and drink, for medicine and for religious ceremonies. They were often very expensive – fitting gifts for a king or for worshipping God.

frankincense tree

myrrh

When the thin bark of the frankincense tree is cut, a greenish resin oozes out. This can be dried and burnt as sweet-smelling incense. The ancient Hebrews used this incense in their worship.

Myrrh is a shrub that gives a pale yellow gum when its stems are cut. It was used as a medicine, a spice and in making holy oil for the temple. It was one of the spices used to embalm Jesus' body.

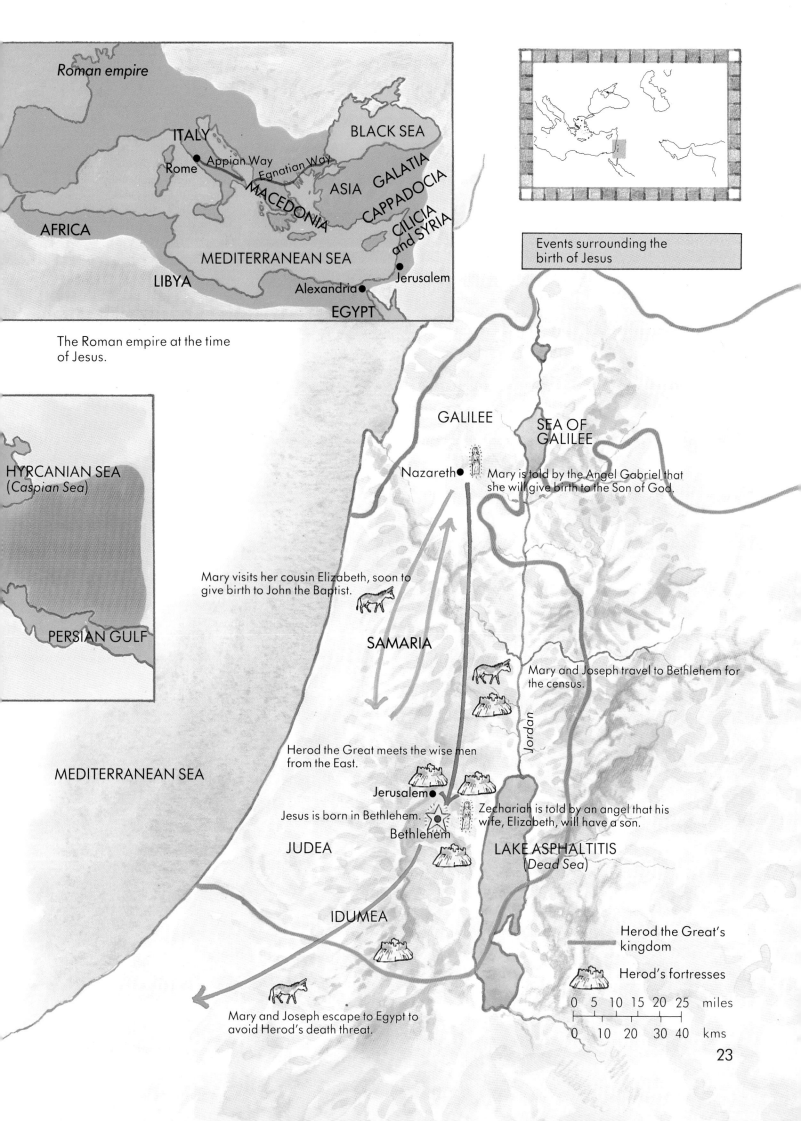

Roman empire

ITALY

Rome ● Appian Way

Egnatian Way

BLACK SEA

MACEDONIA

ASIA

GALATIA

CAPPADOCIA

CILICIA and SYRIA

AFRICA

MEDITERRANEAN SEA

LIBYA

Jerusalem ●

Alexandria ●

EGYPT

The Roman empire at the time of Jesus.

HYRCANIAN SEA
(*Caspian Sea*)

PERSIAN GULF

MEDITERRANEAN SEA

Events surrounding the birth of Jesus

GALILEE

SEA OF GALILEE

Nazareth ● Mary is told by the Angel Gabriel that she will give birth to the Son of God.

Mary visits her cousin Elizabeth, soon to give birth to John the Baptist.

SAMARIA

Mary and Joseph travel to Bethlehem for the census.

Jordan

Herod the Great meets the wise men from the East.

Jerusalem ●

Zechariah is told by an angel that his wife, Elizabeth, will have a son.

Jesus is born in Bethlehem.

Bethlehem

JUDEA

LAKE ASPHALTITIS
(*Dead Sea*)

IDUMEA

Herod the Great's kingdom

Herod's fortresses

0 5 10 15 20 25 miles

0 10 20 30 40 kms

Mary and Joseph escape to Egypt to avoid Herod's death threat.

The life of Jesus

Death and resurrection: *Matthew 21–28; Mark 11–16; Luke 18–24; John 12–21*

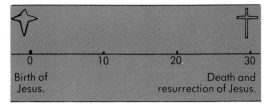

0	10	20	30
Birth of Jesus.			Death and resurrection of Jesus.

Jesus' message is timeless – followed by Christians world-wide today – but knowing about the place and time in which He lived can help us to understand His teaching better.

Jesus taught only for about three years. Most of His teaching took place around the shores of the Sea of Galilee; He spent some time in Judea; and went regularly to Jerusalem for religious festivals.

Jesus knew the history of His people. From His earliest years He studied the Jewish Scriptures. The only glimpse of Jesus as a boy that we have is when He stayed behind in Jerusalem to talk with temple scholars. In His teaching He often quoted from or referred to the Scriptures. He said that He had not come to destroy the religion of the Jews, but to complete it. He taught that trying to keep detailed rules, however good, was not the way to please God and that could only be done by trusting and following Him. To love and serve Him was the beginning of real life with God, which would continue beyond death. Although He did not publicly claim to be the 'Messiah' sent by God, whom the Jewish people were expecting, He did say that He was the 'Son of God' and was related to God in a way in which no one else could ever be. Both His friends and His enemies understood what He meant. This is why His enemies wanted to get rid of Him, and His friends came to believe that He was God, in a way we cannot possibly understand.

Palestine in Jesus' day was an uneasy country. The Roman governors were always worried that there would be an uprising. Anyone with many followers was a threat, and John the Baptist, who was Jesus' cousin, was executed by Herod. The miracles Jesus did showed God's love and alarmed the Jewish authorities even more.

They wanted to get rid of Jesus because He claimed to be the 'Son of God'. They could not execute Him themselves for this because the Roman authorities would not allow it. So they persuaded the Roman Governor, Pontius Pilate, to allow Him to be killed as a rebel against the Emperor. He was beaten and then crucified, which was a very painful and horrible way to die, and was used only to execute the worst criminals.

When Jesus was dead two members of the Jewish Council, who secretly believed that Jesus' claims were true, took His body down from the cross. They covered it with oils and spices, bound it with linen strips, and laid it in a rock tomb. The heavy stone door was then closed, the tomb sealed with the seal of the Roman Governor, and a group of soldiers left to guard it.

A few of Jesus' closest followers came to the tomb early on Sunday morning, the day after the Jewish sabbath. They found the stone door opened, and the body gone, leaving the grave-clothes behind. Then Jesus appeared to His followers on several occasions, including one where 500 were present. Before He returned to heaven, which we call His 'Ascension', He promised that the Holy Spirit would be with His followers always, to spread the 'good news' about Him.

Jesus' body was laid in a rock tomb with a huge stone to seal the entrance. Such tombs can still be seen near Jerusalem today.

Fishers of men

Much of Jesus' life was spent near the Sea of Galilee, where fishing was a major industry, so it is not surprising that He often mentioned fishing in His teaching. At least four of Jesus' disciples were professional fishermen. Lake Galilee is the lowest freshwater lake in the world – over 200 metres (680 feet) below sea level. It is 20 kilometres (13 miles) long and about half as wide. Fishing was done by throwing out a weighted, circular net and using a drawstring to pull the edges together.

The tilapia is also known as 'St Peter's fish'. It is still caught in Lake Galilee and was probably the main catch in New Testament times.

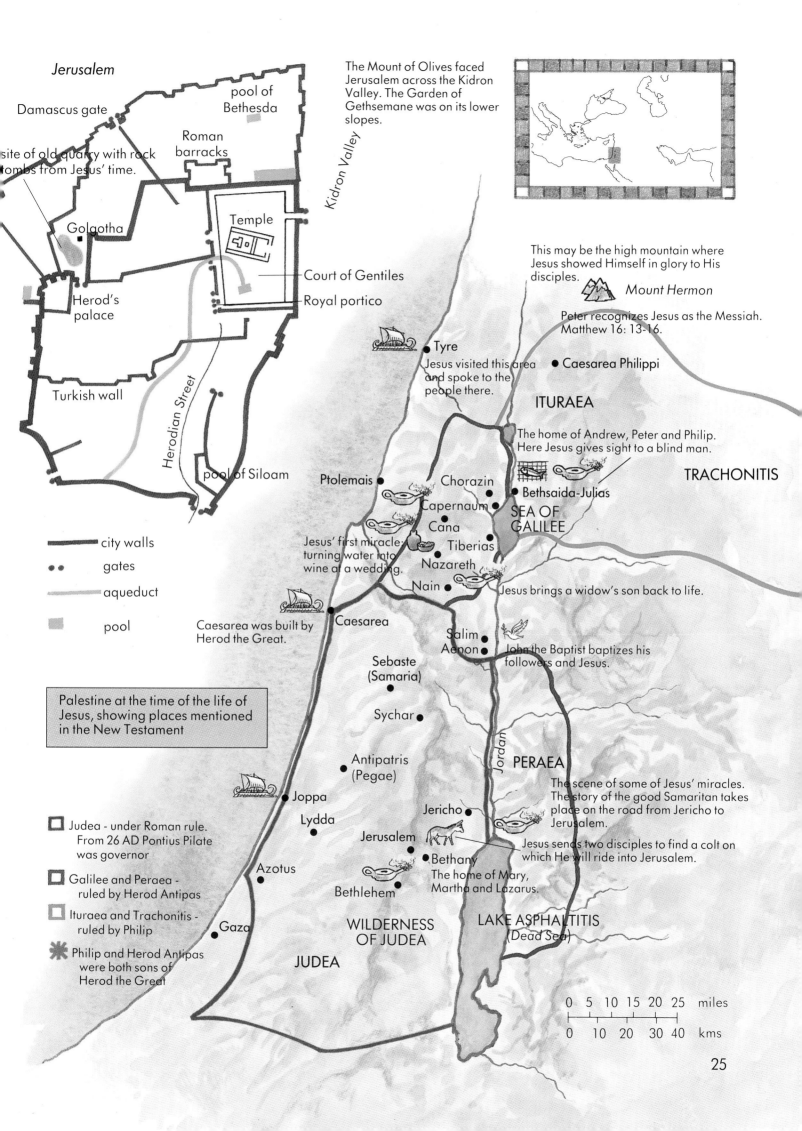

Jerusalem

Damascus gate

pool of Bethesda

site of old quarry with rock tombs from Jesus' time.

Roman barracks

Golgotha

Temple

Court of Gentiles

Royal portico

Herod's palace

Turkish wall

Herodian Street

Kidron Valley

pool of Siloam

The Mount of Olives faced Jerusalem across the Kidron Valley. The Garden of Gethsemane was on its lower slopes.

This may be the high mountain where Jesus showed Himself in glory to His disciples.

Mount Hermon

Peter recognizes Jesus as the Messiah. Matthew 16: 13-16.

Tyre

Jesus visited this area and spoke to the people there.

Caesarea Philippi

ITURAEA

The home of Andrew, Peter and Philip. Here Jesus gives sight to a blind man.

TRACHONITIS

Ptolemais

Chorazin

Capernaum

Bethsaida-Julias

SEA OF GALILEE

Cana

Tiberias

Jesus' first miracle: turning water into wine at a wedding.

Nazareth

Nain

Jesus brings a widow's son back to life.

— city walls

•• gates

— aqueduct

▨ pool

Caesarea was built by Herod the Great.

Caesarea

Salim
Aenon

John the Baptist baptizes his followers and Jesus.

Sebaste (Samaria)

Palestine at the time of the life of Jesus, showing places mentioned in the New Testament

Sychar

Antipatris (Pegae)

Jordan

PERAEA

The scene of some of Jesus' miracles. The story of the good Samaritan takes place on the road from Jericho to Jerusalem.

Joppa

Lydda

Jericho

Jesus sends two disciples to find a colt on which He will ride into Jerusalem.

⬜ Judea - under Roman rule. From 26 AD Pontius Pilate was governor

⬜ Galilee and Peraea - ruled by Herod Antipas

⬜ Ituraea and Trachonitis - ruled by Philip

✳ Philip and Herod Antipas were both sons of Herod the Great

Jerusalem

Bethany

The home of Mary, Martha and Lazarus.

Azotus

Bethlehem

Gaza

WILDERNESS OF JUDEA

LAKE ASPHALTITIS (Dead Sea)

JUDEA

0 5 10 15 20 25 miles

0 10 20 30 40 kms

25

Paul and the early church

Acts; Letters of Paul, Peter, James and John.

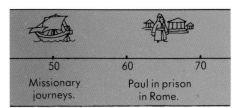

50 Missionary journeys. 60 70 Paul in prison in Rome.

On the day of Pentecost, as usual for a Jewish festival, the disciples were gathered in Jerusalem. Jesus' promise came true when the disciples were filled with the Holy Spirit. Tongues of flame appeared above their heads and, to the astonishment of those present, they found that they could speak easily with people from other countries. At once they began to spread the good news about Jesus. This was the beginning of the Christian church.

The earliest Christians shared all they had with each other. Many people admired them for their way of life and their courage. The authorities, however, were worried about this growing popularity. One of those who persecuted the Christians on behalf of the authorities was a man called Saul.

While on the road to Damascus, in search of Christians to bring to trial, Saul heard the voice of Jesus. He became blind for three days. When he recovered his sight, Saul became a Christian, preaching as fearlessly as those he had once persecuted. Later, he was known as Paul. His missionary journeys were often difficult and dangerous, but he was tireless in spreading the news of Jesus. Several letters written by Paul, teaching, advising and encouraging the new churches, are to be found in the New Testament. There are also letters by other writers, including John, who lived until about 100 AD and died a very old man. Although these letters were written for people whose lives and problems were very different from ours today, they tell us clearly of the truth about Jesus and of the excitement and challenge of living a Christian life.

The Book of Acts vividly describes Paul's voyage to Rome. He travelled on a cargo ship, taking corn to Italy, during some of the roughest sailing months of the year. Egypt's grain was as important to the Roman empire as it had been to the people of Israel in Joseph's time.

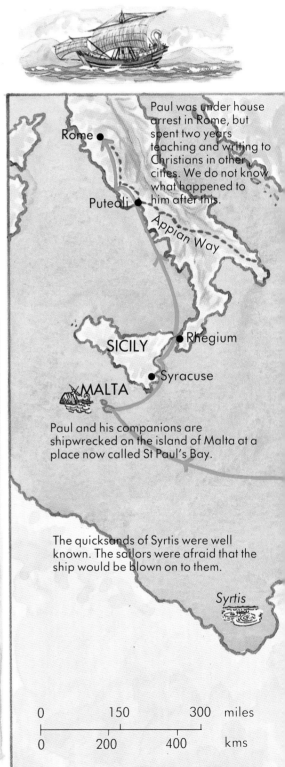

Paul was under house arrest in Rome, but spent two years teaching and writing to Christians in other cities. We do not know what happened to him after this.

Rome
Puteoli
Appian Way
SICILY
Rhegium
Syracuse
MALTA

Paul and his companions are shipwrecked on the island of Malta at a place now called St Paul's Bay.

The quicksands of Syrtis were well known. The sailors were afraid that the ship would be blown on to them.

Syrtis

| 0 | 150 | 300 | miles |
| 0 | 200 | 400 | kms |

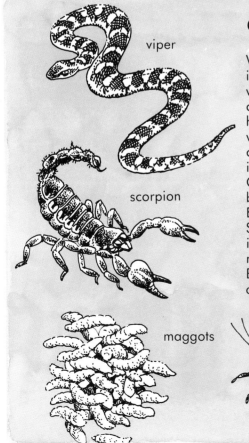

viper

scorpion

maggots

Creeping things

When Paul was shipwrecked on the island of Malta, the local people were astonished to see that a viper, clinging to his hand, did him no harm. This convinced them that Paul was no ordinary man. Other creeping things are also mentioned in the Bible as vivid illustrations of God's power. Swarms of locusts can be terribly destructive, as the Egyptians in Moses' time found. Scorpions live in desert places and it is for their painful sting that they are mentioned in the Bible. When the Bible speaks of 'worms', it is nearly always maggots that are meant.

locust

Rome was the capital of the Roman empire. As a Roman citizen, Paul took advantage of his right to appeal directly to the emperor when he was arrested. His journey to Rome was very eventful and he was met by Christian friends already living there.

The last book of the New Testament is the Book of Revelation, by a writer named John. It was written towards the end of the first century AD. John was in exile on the island of Patmos at a time when Christians were suffering persecution under the Roman emperor, Domitian. It is a book of visions, giving the message that Jesus will triumph over all worldly evil.

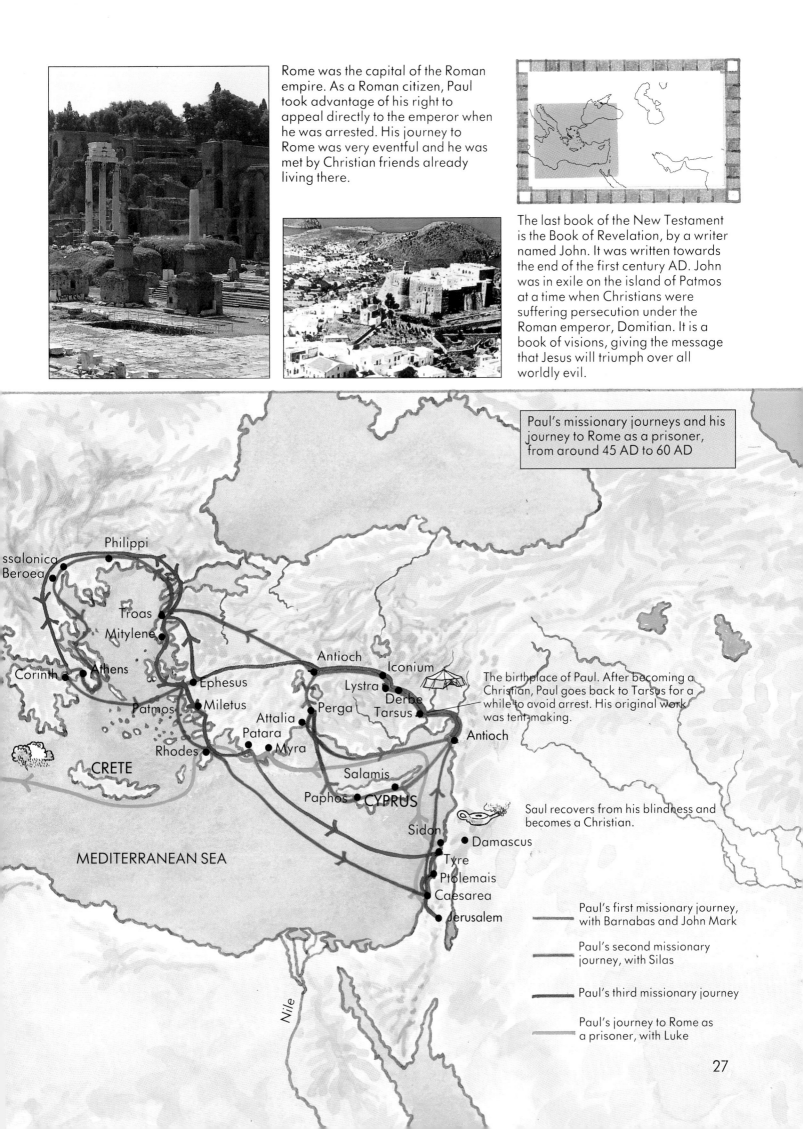

Paul's missionary journeys and his journey to Rome as a prisoner, from around 45 AD to 60 AD

Philippi
ssalonica
Beroea
Troas
Mitylene
Corinth
Athens
Patmos
Ephesus
Miletus
Antioch
Iconium
Lystra
Derbe
Perga
Tarsus
Attalia
Patara
Myra
Rhodes
CRETE
Salamis
Paphos
CYPRUS
Sidon
Damascus
Tyre
Ptolemais
Caesarea
Jerusalem
Antioch
MEDITERRANEAN SEA
Nile

The birthplace of Paul. After becoming a Christian, Paul goes back to Tarsus for a while to avoid arrest. His original work was tent-making.

Saul recovers from his blindness and becomes a Christian.

——— Paul's first missionary journey, with Barnabas and John Mark

——— Paul's second missionary journey, with Silas

——— Paul's third missionary journey

——— Paul's journey to Rome as a prisoner, with Luke

27

Index of places

Abel-beth-maacah town in the north of Palestine 19
Achaia Roman province, now in southern Greece 30
Achshaph town to the west of the Sea of Galilee 15
Adullam town in Judah 21
Aegyptus Roman name for Egypt 30
Aenon place near the River Jordan 25
Africa Roman province in north Africa 23,30
Ai town in Canaan 14,15
Akhetaten capital of Egypt under Pharaoh Akhenaton 2
Alexandria Greek-built port in Egypt 22,30
Ammon area to the east of the River Jordan 15,17,19,21
Antioch town in Pisidia, southern Turkey 27,31
Antipatris town in Samaria, also known as Pegai 25
Arabia land between the Red Sea and the Persian Gulf 3,7,21,31
Arabian Desert desert in what is now Saudi Arabia 7,21,31
Aram area in southern Syria, including Damascus 18,19
Ararat mountain in modern Turkey where the Ark may have come to rest 7
Armenia area now part of Turkey and Iran 21,31
Ashdod Philistine town 21,25
Asia Roman province, now in Turkey 23,30
Asphaltitis Greek name for the Dead Sea 21,23,25
Assyria area of northern Mesopotamia from which the Assyrian empire grew 3,19
Athens capital of Greece 2,22,27,30
Attalia port in southern Turkey 27
Azekah town in Judah 21
Azotus Greek name for Ashdod 25

Baalath town in Canaan 17
Babel city, probably Babylon, where a great tower was built 9
Babylon city on River Euphrates, capital of Babylonia 3,9,19,20,21,22,31
Babylonia area in southern Mesopotamia from which the Babylonian empire grew 3,9,21
Bactria north-east part of the Persian empire 21
Beersheba town in the south of Judea 9,11,19,21
Beroea town in northern Greece 27
Bethany place near Jerusalem 25
Bethel town in Canaan, scene of many Old Testament events 9,10,11,15,19
Beth-horon valley city north-west of Jerusalem 17
Bethlehem town near Jerusalem, birthplace of David and Jesus 11, 16,17,22,23,25
Bethphage place near Jerusalem 25
Bethsaida-Julias town on shores of the Sea of Galilee 25
Bithynia Roman province south of the Black Sea 30
Bitter Lakes marshy lakes above the western arm of the Red Sea 13
Brundisium Roman port in south Italy 30
Byzantium city in Turkey, now Istanbul 30

Caesarea Roman port on the coast of Palestine 25,27,31
Caesarea Philippi Roman town at the source of the River Jordan 25
Cana village in Galilee 25
Canaan country promised by God to the Israelites in which they settled 8,9,10, 11,13,14,15
Capernaum town on the Sea of Galilee 25
Cappadocia Roman province, now eastern Turkey 23,31
Carchemish city in northern Syria on the River Euphrates 2,21
Carmel one of a range of hills near the coast west of the Sea of Galilee 19
Carthage capital of Roman province of Africa 30
Chinnereth early name for the Sea of Galilee 17,19
Chorazin town in Galilee 25
Cilicia Roman province, now southern Turkey 23,31
Colossae town in what is now Turkey 30
Corinth city in southern Greece 2,27,30
Corsica Mediterranean island, west of Italy 30
Crete island in the eastern Mediterranean 2,7,27,30
Cyprus island in the eastern Mediterranean 2,27,30
Cyrenaica region in northern Libya 30
Cyrene town in Cyrenaica 30

Dalmatia Roman province, now in Yugoslavia 30
Damascus city in Syria 2,17,19,21,26,27,31
Dan place where the tribe of the same name settled 19
Danube river in Europe 2,3,30
Dead Sea sea into which the River Jordan runs, with high salt content 2,11,13,15, 17,19,21,23,25
Decapolis name in Roman times for area containing 10 cities east of River Jordan 31
Debir town in Canaan 15
Derbe town in southern Turkey 27
Dor town in Canaan 17
Dothan place in Canaan 11

Edom area to the south of the Dead Sea, later Idumea 10,11,13,15,17,19,21
Eglon town in Canaan 15
Egypt powerful country to the south-west of Israel 2,8,9,10,11,12,13,17,18,19, 21,22,23,27,31
En-rimmon town in Judah 21
Ephah town in north-west Arabia 2
Ephesus capital of Roman province of Asia, now western Turkey 21,27,30
Ephraim place where the tribe of the same name settled 15
Ephrath earlier name for Bethlehem 11
Euphrates important river in Mesopotamia 3,7,9,19,31
Ezion-geber also known as Elath, town at the top of the eastern arm of the Red Sea 2,13

Galatia Roman province, now central Turkey 23,31

Galilee lake in Palestine (also known as Chinnereth or Gennesaret) and the district to the west of it 23,24,25,31
Gaza Philistine town south-west of Jerusalem 2,17,19,25
Geba town in Judea 21
Gennesaret name for Sea of Galilee 25
Gezer town in Canaan 17
Gibbethon town west of Jerusalem 19
Gibeon town near Jerusalem 15,21
Gilead area east of the River Jordan 11
Gilgal place near Jericho where the Israelites crossed the Jordan 15
Gittaim town in Judah 21
Goshen area in Egypt east of the River Nile 11,13
Great Sea ancient name for the Mediterranean Sea 2,7,9,11,13,15,21
Greece country from which the Greek empire grew 22

Hadid town in Judah 21
Haran town to the north of Israel in Paddan-aram area 3,9,11,21
Hazar-shual town in Judah 21
Hazor important Canaanite city north of Sea of Galilee 15,17,21
Hebron town in Judea 8,9,11,15,21
Heraclea Black Sea port 30
Hermon mountain in Ituraea, source of the River Jordan 25
Hindush eastern part of the Persian empire, now in India 21
Horeb mountain on Sinai peninsula 19
Hyrcanian Sea Greek name for the Caspian Sea 23,31

Iconium town in southern Turkey 27
Idumea name for Edom after the exile 21,23
Illyricum Roman province, now in Yugoslavia 30
Israel name which God gave to Jacob, also applied to Jacob's descendants and the land they lived in, also the northern kingdom when Israel and Judah were split 13,14,15,16,17,18, 19,20,27
Italy centre of the Roman empire 23,26,30
Ituraea area north-east of Sea of Galilee ruled by Philip 25
Iyyon town north of Dan 19

Jarmuth town south-west of Jerusalem 15,21
Jericho important city north of the Dead Sea 13,14,15,25
Jerusalem city to the west of the Dead Sea, capital of Judah, centre of Jewish worship 2,15,16,17,19,20,21, 22,23,24,25,26,27,31
Jeshua town in Judah 21
Jezreel town in northern Israel 19
Joppa port on the coast of Israel 17,19,25
Jordan main river of Israel, passing through Sea of Galilee and Dead Sea 2,7,11,14,15,17,19,21,23,25
Judah name of the southern kingdom when Israel was divided 18,19,20,21
Judea Greek and Roman name for Judah 23,24,25,31

Kadesh-barnea oasis in the desert south-west of the Dead Sea 13

Kiriath-arba town in Judah, another name for Hebron 21

Lachish town south of Jerusalem 15,21
Lebanon country north of Israel 17
Libya area of northern Africa 2,23,30
Lod town in Judah 21,25
Lower Sea the Persian Gulf 21
Lycia Roman province, now in south-west Turkey 30
Lydda Roman name for Lod 25
Lydia area in what is now Turkey 21
Lystra town in southern Turkey 27

Macedonia Roman province, now northern Greece 22,23,30
Madon town to the west of the Sea of Galilee 15
Mahanaim place east of the Jordan 11
Makkedah town south-west of Jerusalem 15
Malta Mediterranean island 26,30
Manasseh tribe descended from Joseph and the area where they settled 15
Mare Internum Roman name for Mediterranean Sea 30,31
Mari important city in Babylonia 3
Media country to the east of the River Tigris, now part of Iran 3,21,22
Mediterranean sea bordering Europe, Africa and the Middle East, known in ancient times as the Great Sea 2,7,9,11,13,15,21,22,23,25,27,30,31
Megiddo city in Canaan 17,19
Memphis once capital of Egypt 2,21
Merom Canaanite town north of the Sea of Galilee 15
Mesopotamia the land around the Rivers Euphrates and Tigris 7,31
Michmash town in Judah 21
Midian area of west Arabia 12,13
Miletus port in western Turkey 27,30
Mitylene port on island of Lesbos off Turkish coast 27
Moab area to the east of the Dead Sea 13,15,17,19,21
Moladah town in Judah 21
Myra port in southern Turkey 27

Nain place in Galilee 25
Nazareth town in Galilee that Mary and Joseph came from 23,25
Neballat town in Judah 21
Nebo mountain east of the Dead Sea 13
Negeb Desert desert area in south of Israel, sometimes spelt 'Negev' 7,9,11,13
Nile important river on which Egypt's economy depended 2,7,9,10,11,12,13,19,21,27,30
Nineveh capital of Assyria 3,19
Numidia Roman province in north-west Africa 30

Olives, Mount of hill outside Jerusalem 25
On city in Egypt, later called Heliopolis 2,11
Ono place to the south of Samaria 21
Ostia Roman port in Italy 30
Oxus river now called Amu Darya and in the USSR 21

Paddan-aram area to the north of Israel from which Rebecca and Rachel came 9,10,11

Palestine name for the land of the Philistines that came to refer to a wider area 15,17,21,23,24
Paphos town in Cyprus 27,30
Parthia part of Persian empire south of the Caspian sea 21,31
Patara place in southern Turkey 27
Patmos island off the coast of Turkey 27
Pegae name for Antipatris 25
Penuel place east of the River Jordan 11,19
Peraea Roman province east of River Jordan 25,31
Perga port in southern Turkey 27
Pergamum town in what is now western Turkey 30
Persepolis capital of Persia at the time of Darius 21
Persia country east of the River Tigris 21
Persian Gulf sea into which the Rivers Tigris and Euphrates flow 3,7,21,23,31
Petra desert city south-east of Judea 31
Pharos island near port later called Alexandria 2
Philadelphia town in what is now Turkey 30
Philippi place in northern Greece 27
Philistia land of the Philistines to the south-west of Judah 19
Phrygia area now in western Turkey 30
Pisidia area now in central Turkey 30
Pithom store-city in Egypt built by Hebrew slaves 13
Pontus Roman province south of the Black Sea 31
Pontus Euxinus Roman name for the Black Sea 30
Ptolemais Mediterranean port south of Tyre 25,27
Puteoli Roman port in Italy 26,30

Rabbah capital of Ammon 17
Ramah town north of Jerusalem 19,21
Rameses store-city in Egypt built by Hebrew slaves 13
Ramoth-gilead city east of the River Jordan 18,19
Red Sea in Hebrew 'the sea of reeds'; sea between Africa and Arabia; also used for the area in north Egypt crossed by the Israelites 2,7,13,21,31
Rephidim place on Sinai peninsula where Israelites beat Amalekites 13
Rhegium Roman port in Italy 26
Rhodes Mediterranean island and its main city 2,27,30
Rome capital of the Roman empire 23,26,27,30

Salamis town in Cyprus 27
Salim place near the River Jordan 25
Salt Sea ancient name for the Dead Sea, which is surrounded by land and contains a high level of salt 2,11,13,15,17,19
Samaria capital of northern kingdom of Israel, and the area around it 17,19,21,23,25
Sardinia Mediterranean island, west of Italy 30
Sardis town in what is now western Turkey 30
Sebaste Roman name for Samaria 25
Sheba country south of Israel whose queen visited Solomon 17

Shechem important town in Canaan 9,11,15,17,19
Shiloh town north of Jerusalem 16,17,19
Shimron town to the west of the Sea of Galilee 15
Shittim place east of the River Jordan 15
Sicily island south of Italy 26,30
Sidon Mediterranean port north of Tyre 17,19,27
Sinai mountain on the peninsula of the same name where Moses received the Ten Commandments, probably Mount Horeb 12,13
Smyrna town in what is now western Turkey 2,30
St Paul's Bay port on island of Malta 27
Succoth two places: town east of the River Jordan 11,17; place east of the Nile delta 13
Susa city east of the River Tigris 3,20,21
Sychar Samaritan town 25
Syracuse town in Sicily 26,30
Syria country north of Israel 22,23,31
Syrian Desert desert north-east of Israel 7
Syrtis quicksands off the coast of Africa 26

Tamar town in Edom, south of the Dead Sea 17
Tarentum port in southern Italy 30
Tarsus town now in southern Turkey 2,27,31
Tema city in Arabia 21
Thebes once capital of Egypt 2,21
Thessalonica area of northern Greece 27
Thrace Roman province, now in northern Greece 22,30
Tiberias Roman town on the shores of the Sea of Galilee 25
Tigris important river in Mesopotamia 3,7,9,31
Tirzah first capital of the northern kingdom of Israel 19
Tishbe birthplace in Gilead of Elijah 19
Trachonitis area east of Ituraea ruled by Philip 25
Troas port in north-west Turkey 27
Tyre Mediterranean port in Lebanon, north of Israel 2,17,19,25,27
Tyrrhenian Sea sea between Italy and Sardinia 30

Ugarit city north of Canaan 2
Ur great Mesopotamian city, birthplace of Abram 3,7,9,19
Urmia lake now in Iran 3,31

Van lake now in Turkey 3,31

Western Desert ancient name for what is now the Libyan Desert 7
Wilderness of Judea desert area west of the Dead Sea 25
Wilderness of Paran desert area near Kadesh-barnea 13
Wilderness of Shur desert area in the north of the Sinai peninsula 13
Wilderness of Sin desert area in the south of the Sinai peninsula 13

Zanoah town in Judah 21
Zarephath town near Sidon 19
Zarethan town east of the River Jordan 17
Ziklag town in Judah 21
Zorah town in Judah 21

The New Testament World

ITALY

CORSICA

SARDINIA

Rome
Ostia

Puteoli · Appian Way
Tarentum · Brundisium

TYRRHENIAN SEA

SICILY

Syracuse

Carthage

MALTA

AFRICA

ILLYRICUM
(Dalmatia)

Danube

THRACE

Egnatian Way

MACEDONIA

Byzantium · Heraclea

BITHYNIA AND PONTU

PONTUS EUXINUS
(Black Sea)

GALATIA

ASIA

PHRYGIA

Pergamum

Smyrna · Sardis

Ephesus · Philadelphia

Colossae

Athens

Corinth

ACHAIA

Miletus

PISIDIA

Tars

LYCIA

Rhodes

CRETE

CYPRUS

Paphos

MARE INTERNUM
(Mediterranean Sea)

GALILEE

Caesarea
Jerusale

JUD

Cyrene

CYRENAICA

LIBYA

Alexandria

AEGYPTUS

Nile

RED
SEA

AD	0	10	20	30	40	50	60	70	80	90
	Birth of Jesus.			Death and resurrection of Jesus.		Missionary journeys.	Paul in prison in Rome.			Book of Revelation written.